QUOTED MOMENTS

COMPILED BY JOANNE MALONEY

in aid of **irish cancer society**

CallSave 1850 60 60 60
www.cancer.ie

FIRST PUBLISHED IN 2011

COPYRIGHT: JOANNE MALONEY, BOHESS, ISLANDEADY, CASTLEBAR, CO. MAYO, IRELAND
PUBLISHER: JOANNE MALONEY, BOHESS, ISLANDEADY, CASTLEBAR, CO. MAYO, IRELAND
DESIGN: KEY MEDIA DESIGN, LOUISBURGH, CO. MAYO, IRELAND
PRINTING: KPS COLOUR PRINT, KNOCK, CO. MAYO, IRELAND

ISBN   978-0-9568993-0-9

A SPECIAL THANK YOU MUST BE EXTENDED TO THE FOLLOWING COMPANIES FOR THEIR GENEROUS CONTRIBUTIONS TO THIS PROJECT

PRINTING: KPS COLOUR PRINT
PAPER: SWAN PAPER
INK: GRAPHOCOLOR
PLATES: TYPETEC

Dedicated with love to

Mum & Linda

My Shining Stars

The journey of a thousand miles

begins with a *single step*

- Lao Tzu

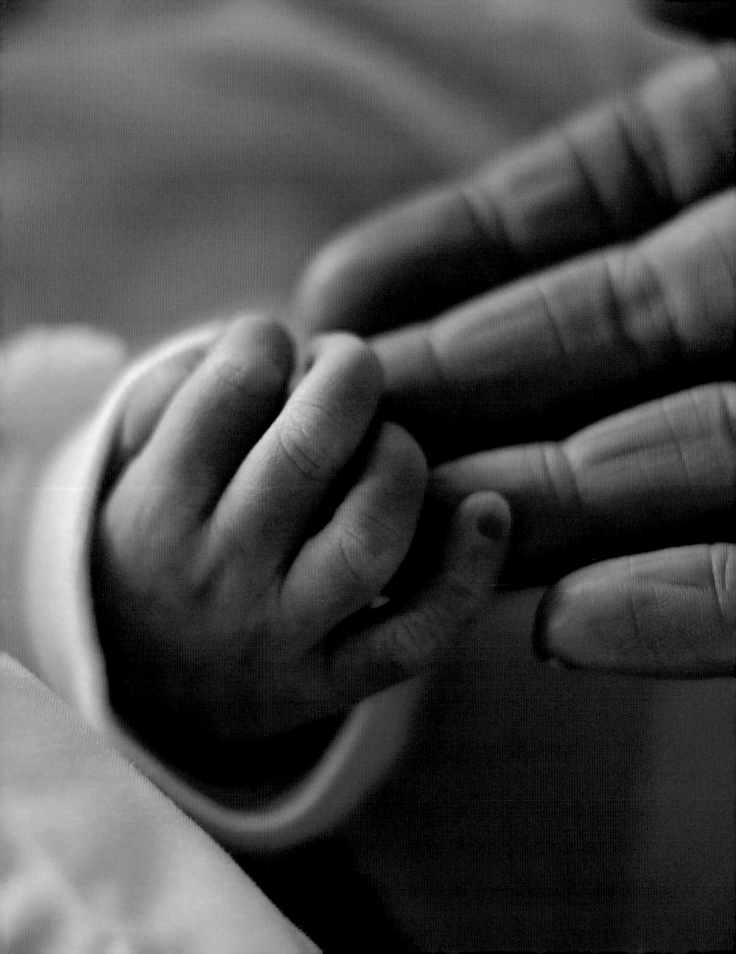

A baby is born with

a need to be loved

and never outgrows it

- FRANK A. CLARK

There are no

seven wonders

of the world

in the eyes of a child.

There are seven million

Live Your Best Life Now

God's people should be the happiest on earth
Filled with harmony, peace and mirth
A fabulous future coming our way
If we can only enjoy life everyday

Don't just go through the motions in life
Feeling empty, unhappy, dissatisfied
Trudging through life trying to please everyone
Neglecting the needs of "Number One"

Lacking enthusiasm, never being excited
A sign that we are not contented
Welcome God our way
We'll see beauty every day
His greatest gifts are all around
In this garden of Eden they abound

What a wonderful gift we have been given
This masterpiece of Creation to live in
When we find love and peace within our heart
Only then will we see God's work of art

Live life with passion, do everything with our whole heart
Rekindle that inner fire, show others where to start
Raise our level of expectancy
Faith will activate the power of God
Who will take us to places we've never dreamed of.

- ANTOINETTE KEANE

He who would learn to fly
one day must first learn to
stand and walk and run
and climb and dance;
one cannot fly into flying

- FRIEDRICH NIETZSCHE

Adopt the pace of nature:

her secret is patience

- RALPH WALDO EMERSON

The trees that are
slow to grow
bear the best fruit

– MOLIERE

In matters of style,
swim with the current;
in matters of principle,
stand like a rock

– THOMAS JEFFERSON

It isn't the mountains
ahead to climb
that wear you out;
it's the pebble
in your shoe

- MUHAMMAD ALI

To be yourself in a world that is constantly trying to make you something else is the greatest accomplishment

- RALPH WALDO EMERSON

You can't cross the sea merely

by standing and staring at the water

- RABINDRANATH TAGORE

The only real voyage
of discovery consists
not in seeking new landscapes
but in having new eyes

— MARCEL PROUST

Do not follow

where the path may lead.

Go instead

where there is

no path and leave a trail

– RALPH WALDO EMERSON

The fishermen know
that the sea is dangerous
and the storm terrible, but
they have never found these
dangers sufficient reason
for remaining ashore

- Vincent Van Gogh

With the new day
comes new strength
and new thoughts

— ELEANOR ROOSEVELT

Only those who will risk going too far

can possibly find out

how far one can go

- T S E<small>LIOT</small>

The same fence that

shuts others out

shuts you in

- BILL COPELAND

It Could Be Worse

We all hit on a bad day
Where darkness blocks our light
A day that's filled with obstacles
Where nothing will go right.
A day when we receive bad news
And all our hope seems gone
When we feel like throwing in the towel
It's that hard to struggle on.
That's the day to take some time out
And open up our mind
And to spare a thought for others
That the world has left behind.
Some will starve of hunger
Because their lands are parched and dry
They have no means to feed their families
So they watch their children die.
Some are forced to work as slaves
A life without a choice
They come and go through this world
And they never have a voice.
Some live their lives in torture
Their screams fall on deaf ears
Each morning they wake up to
Another day of tears.
If all our days were bad days
And thank God that isn't true
There are millions still would gladly swap
Their lives with me and you.

Keep your face to the

sunshine and you

cannot see the shadow

- HELEN KELLER

The best remedy for those
who are afraid, lonely
or unhappy is to go outside,
somewhere where they can be quiet,
alone with the heavens, nature and God.
Because only then does one feel
that all is as it should be.

- ANNE FRANK

The greatest *glory in living*

lies not in never falling,

but in rising *every time we* fall

– Nelson Mandela

Courage is not

the towering oak

that sees storms

come and go;

it is the fragile blossom

that opens in the snow

- ALICE MACKENZIE SWAIM

To get through

the hardest *journey*

we need take only one step

at a time

but we must

keep on stepping

- CHINESE PROVERB

The way I see it,

if you want

the rainbow,

you gotta put up

with the rain

- DOLLY PARTON

Believe in yourself
and all that you are.
Know that there is something
inside you that is
greater than any **obstacle.**

– CHRISTIAN D. LARSON

If you are going through hell,

keep going

– WINSTON CHURCHILL

When one door
of happiness *closes*,

another *opens*;

but often we look so long

at the closed door

that we do not see the one

which has been opened

for us

- HELEN KELLER

For every minute

you are ANGRY

you lose *sixty seconds*

of happiness

– RALPH WALDO EMERSON

When you lose,

don't lose the lesson

- UNKNOWN

You cannot train a horse

with shouts and expect it

to obey a whisper

- DAGOBERT D RUNES

No one can make you feel inferior

without your consent

\- Eleanor Roosevelt

One reason why birds
and horses are happy
is because they are not
trying to impress other
birds and horses

- DALE CARNEGIE

If you don't

know where

you are going,

any road will

get you there

– Lewis Carroll

In order for the light

to shine so brightly,

the darkness must be present.

- FRANCIS BACON, SR.

Faith is taking the first step even when you don't see the whole *staircase*

- MARTIN LUTHER KING, JR.

I'm not afraid of storms

for I'm learning how to sail my ship

- LOUISA MAY ALCOTT

Tomorrow Is A New Day

Today is just another day

It will come and it will go

And depending on the way you feel

It might pass fast or slow.

It might be very special

The best day you've ever had

Or you might be at a low ebb

Alone, grieving and sad.

One thing you can be sure of

Which ever one it is

Changes keep on happening.

Life won't stay like this.

No matter what you're going through

This feeling will not last

The sun will rise tomorrow

And today will be the past.

- PETER COSTELLO

The cave
you *fear* to enter
holds the *treasure*
you *seek*

– JOSEPH CAMPBELL

Three grand essentials to happiness in this life are something to do, something to love, and something to hope for

- JOSEPH ADDISON

Every blade of grass
has its *angel*
that bends over it
and *whispers,*
'Grow, grow'

- THE TALMUD

Don't walk in front of me
I may not follow
Don't walk behind me
I may not lead

*Walk beside me
and be my friend*

- ALBERT CAMUS

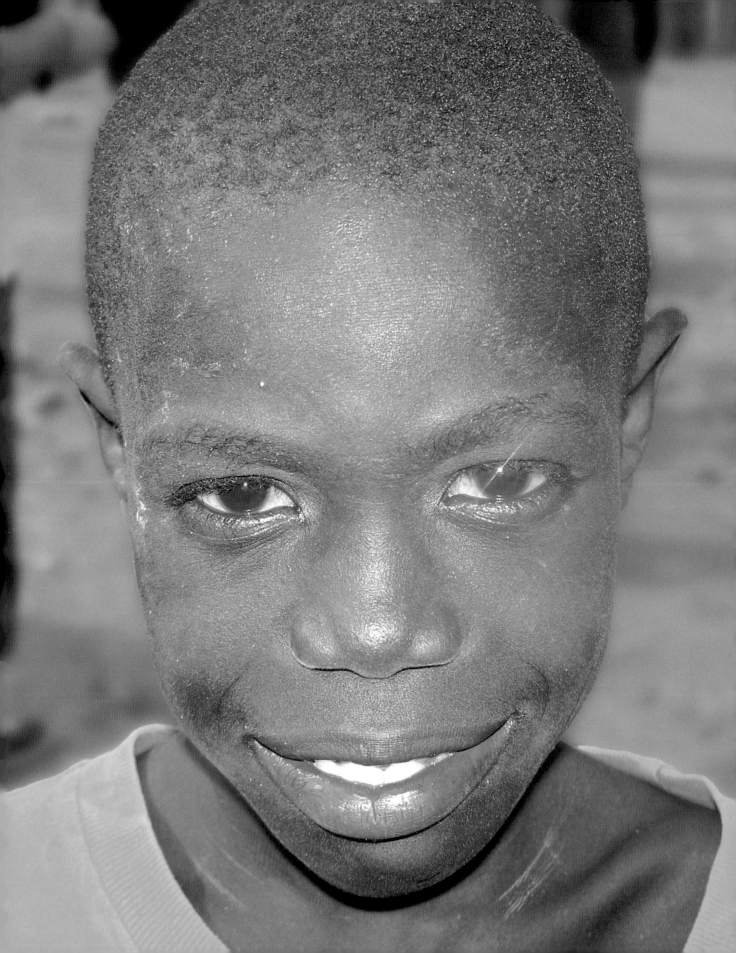

A warm smile

is the

universal language

of kindness

- WILLIAM ARTHUR WARD

May God grant you always...
A sunbeam to warm you,
a moonbeam to charm you,
a sheltering Angel
so nothing can harm you.
Laughter to cheer you.
Faithful friends near you.
And whenever you pray,
Heaven to hear you

- IRISH BLESSING

Remember that *silence is*

sometimes the best *answer*

– Dalai Lama

Every time you
smile at someone,
it is an action of love,
a gift to that person,
a beautiful thing

- MOTHER TERESA

It's the friends

you can call up

at 4 a.m. that matter

— MARLENE DIETRICH

At times our own light
goes out and is rekindled by
a spark from another person.
Each of us has cause to
think with deep gratitude
of those who have lit
the flame within us.

- ALBERT SCHWEITZER

Love does not consist in

gazing at each other,

but in looking

outward together

in the same direction

- ANTOINE DE SAINT-EXUPÉRY

Individually, we are one drop.

Together, we are an ocean.

- RYUNOSUKE SATORO

Today a reader,

tomorrow a leader

- MARGARET FULLER

And the day came

when the risk it took

to remain tight inside

the bud was more painful than

the risk it took to blossom

- ANAIS NIN

Far away there in the sunshine
are my highest aspirations.
I may not reach them,
but I can look up
and see their beauty,
believe in them,
and try to follow
where they lead.

- LOUISA MAY ALCOTT

The man who

has no imagination

has no wings

- MUHAMMAD ALI

A bird doesn't sing

because it has an answer,

it sings because it has a ꜱᴏɴɢ

- Mᴀʏᴀ Aɴɢᴇʟᴏᴜ

People travel to wonder
at the height of the mountains,
at the huge waves of the seas,
at the long course of the rivers,
at the vast compass of the ocean,
at the circular motion of the stars,
and yet they pass by themselves
without wondering

— St. Augustine

Be able to be alone.
Lose not the advantage
of solitude

- THOMAS BROWNE

God grant me the serenity

To accept the things

I cannot change;

Courage to change

the things I can;

And wisdom to know

the difference

- Reinhold Niebuhr

When you come to the

end of your rope,

tie a knot and

hang on..

— FRANKLIN D. ROOSEVELT

Where I live if someone gives you

a hug it's from the heart

- STEVE IRWIN

*You cannot be lonely
if you like the person
you're alone with*

– Wayne Dyer

Twenty years from now
you will be more disappointed
by the things that you didn't do
than by the ones you did do.
So throw off the bowlines.
Sail away from the safe harbour.
Catch the trade winds in your sails.
Explore. Dream. Discover.

- MARK TWAIN

Life is the flower

for which love

is the honey

- Victor Hugo

Hope is the thing with feathers,

that perches in the soul,

and sings the tune without words,

and never stops at all

– EMILY DICKINSON

When you've got something to prove,

there's nothing greater than a challenge

– TERRY BRADSHAW

I hated every minute of training, but I said, "Don't quit. Suffer now and live the rest of your life as a champion."

- MUHAMMAD ALI

Winners take time

to relish their work,

knowing that scaling the mountain

is what makes the view

from the top so exhilarating.

- DENIS WAITLEY

Everything has its beauty,

but not everyone sees it

- CONFUCIUS

Life is an opportunity,
benefit from it.
Life is beauty, admire it.
Life is bliss, taste it.
Life is a dream, realize it.
Life is a challenge, meet it.
Life is a duty, complete it.
Life is a game, play it.
Life is a promise, fulfill it.
Life is sorrow, overcome it.
Life is a song, sing it.
Life is a struggle, accept it.
Life is a tragedy, confront it.
Life is an adventure, dare it.
Life is luck, make it.
Life is too precious,
do not destroy it.
Life is life, fight for it.

— MOTHER TERESA

All alone in a place of wide wide spaces,

man finds his soul

- Ric J Steininger

The true meaning of life

is to plant trees,

under whose shade you

do not expect to sit

– NELSON HENDERSON

Why don't you climb

down off the cross,

take the wood

to build a bridge,

and get over it!

- CHRISTOPHER TITUS

When you get the choice

to sit it out or dance,

I hope you dance

– LEE ANN WOMACK

When you find

peace within yourself,

you become the kind of person

who can live at peace with others

- PEACE PILGRIM

Love doesn't make the world go round,

love is what makes the ride worthwhile

– FRANKLIN P. JONES

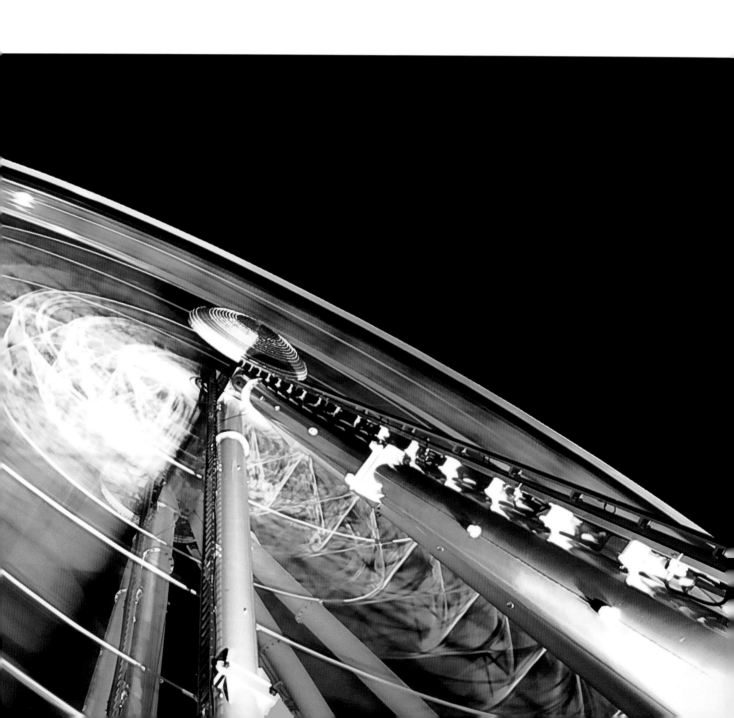

A pearl is a beautiful thing
that is produced by an injured life.
It is the tear that results
from the injury of the oyster.
The treasure of our being
in this world is also produced
by an injured life.
If we had not been wounded,
if we had not been injured,
then we will not produce the pearl.

- STEPHAN HOELLER

Knowing others
is wisdom,
knowing yourself
is Enlightenment

- LAO TZU

God gave us our memories so that we might have roses in December

- JAMES M BARRIE

Life is not about waiting

for the storm to pass...

It's about learning how

to dance in the rain

- VIVIAN GREENE

Don't let anyone else take the measure of your worth and capabilities.

Always stand proud in who you are!

– Margaret Spellings

Best Things In Life Are Free

Did you ever stop and wonder
About this beauty that is ours
The green fields and the mountains
The sunshine and the showers.
The smell of scented heather
The bright fresh evening breeze
The beating waves the golden sands
Or the splendour of the trees.
Our lovely lakes and rivers
The larks up in the sky
And all those priceless treasures
That money cannot buy.
Sometimes we don't appreciate
If we're not charged a fee
Wake up and smell the coffee
The best things in life are free

- PETER COSTELLO

Some people

come into our lives and quickly go.

Some stay for a while,

leave footprints on our hearts,

And we are never, ever the same.

- FLAVIA WEEDN

When you make

the finding *yourself* -

even if you're the last person

on Earth to see the *light* -

you'll never *forget* it

- CARL SAGAN

There are only two ways
to live your life.
One is as though
nothing is a miracle.
The other is as though
everything is a miracle.

– ALBERT EINSTEIN

A good traveller has no fixed plans,

and is not intent *on arriving*

- Lao Tzu

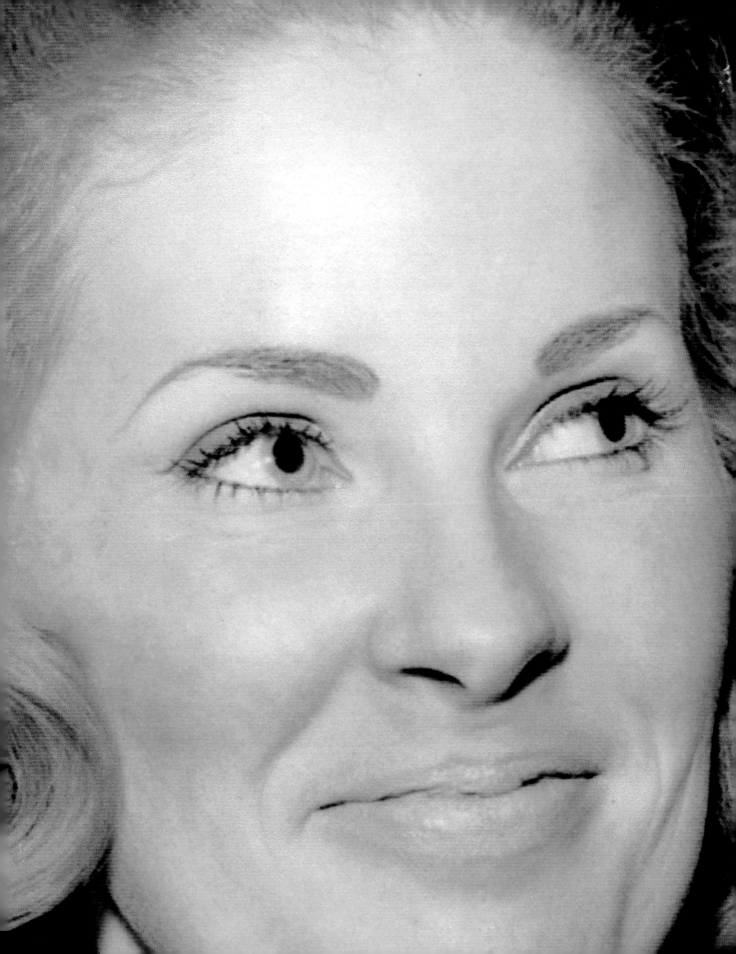

For beautiful eyes,

look for the good in others;

for beautiful lips,

speak only words of kindness;

and for poise,

walk with the knowledge

that you are never alone

- AUDREY HEPBURN

I would rather be ashes than dust!
I would rather that my spark
should burn out in a brilliant blaze
than it should be stifled by dry-rot.
I would rather be a superb meteor,
every atom of me in magnificent glow,
than a sleepy and permanent planet.
The proper function of man
is to live, not to exist.
I shall not waste my days
in trying to prolong them.
I shall use my time.

- JACK LONDON

Life is a great
big CANVAS,
and you should
throw all the PAINT
on it you can

- DANNY KAYE

Always keep that happy attitude. Pretend that you are holding a beautiful fragrant bouquet.

- CANDICE M. POPE

Clouds come floating into my life,

no longer to carry rain or usher storm,

but to add colour to my sunset sky

- RABINDRANATH TAGORE

If the only prayer

you said in your whole life was,

Thank You,

that would suffice

- MEISTER ECKHART

To leave the world a bit better ...

to know that one life

has breathed easier

because you have lived.

This is to have succeeded.

- Ralph Waldo Emerson

It's good to have an *end* to journey towards;

but it's the journey *that matters, in the end*

- URSULA K LEGUIN

PHOTO CONTRIBUTORS

 **– MATT LOUGHREY**
WWW.CROAGHPATRICK365.COM

 – KERSTIN HELLMANN
WWW.KEYMEDIAPHOTOGRAPHY.COM

 **– JIM STAPLETON**
WWW.FLICKR.COM/PHOTOS/JIMSTAPLETON

 – WARREN DOWLING
THEDOWLINGFAMILY@GMAIL.COM

 **– DICKON WHITEHEAD**
WWW.DICKONWHITEHEAD.COM

 – BRIAN DWYER
WWW.IMAGESBYBRIAN.NET

 **– KERSTIN HELLMANN**
WWW.KEYMEDIAPHOTOGRAPHY.COM

 – KERSTIN HELLMANN
WWW.KEYMEDIAPHOTOGRAPHY.COM

 **– BRIAN DWYER**
WWW.IMAGESBYBRIAN.NET

 – MATT LOUGHREY
WWW.CROAGHPATRICK365.COM

 **– DICKON WHITEHEAD**
WWW.DICKONWHITEHEAD.COM

 – KERSTIN HELLMANN
WWW.KEYMEDIAPHOTOGRAPHY.COM

 – JOHN ROCHE
OB1SCOBY@GMAIL.COM

 – LORRAINE MCENIRY
LANIEMC@HOTMAIL.COM

 – BEN WRAFTER
WRAFTER@IOL.IE

 – DECLAN COURELL
WWW.DECLANCOURELLPHOTOGRAPHY.COM

 – MATT LOUGHREY
WWW.CROAGHPATRICK365.COM

 – NOEL BROWNE
WWW.NOELBROWNEPHOTOGRAPHER.COM

 – STEPHEN MURRAY
WWW.STEPHENMURRAY.CARBONMADE.COM

 – NOEL BROWNE
WWW.NOELBROWNEPHOTOGRAPHER.COM

– JOHN MEE
WWW.JOHNMEEPHOTOGRAPHY.COM

 – AAFKE BAKKER
WWW.AMOSTLIKEABLEPLACE.WORDPRESS.COM

Photo Contributors

- Matt Loughrey
WWW.CROAGHPATRICK365.COM

- Brian Dwyer
WWW.IMAGESBYBRIAN.NET

- Matt Loughrey
WWW.CROAGHPATRICK365.COM

- Dickon Whitehead
WWW.DICKONWHITEHEAD.COM

- Sarah Keane
KEANESARAH@MSN.COM

- Brian Dwyer
WWW.IMAGESBYBRIAN.NET

- Noel Browne
WWW.NOELBROWNEPHOTOGRAPHER.COM

- Darren Moran
WWW.DARRENMORANPHOTOGRAPHY.COM

- Brian Dwyer
WWW.IMAGESBYBRIAN.NET

- Celia Anderson
WWW.SHUTTERSTOCK.COM/G/CHATTERBOX

- Declan Courell
WWW.DECLANCOURELLPHOTOGRAPHY.COM

- John Mee
WWW.JOHNMEEPHOTOGRAPHY.COM

- Sarah Keane
KEANESARAH@MSN.COM

- Dickon Whitehead
WWW.DICKONWHITEHEAD.COM

- Noel Browne
WWW.NOELBROWNEPHOTOGRAPHER.COM

- Lorraine McEniry
LANIEMC@HOTMAIL.COM

- Brian Dwyer
WWW.IMAGESBYBRIAN.NET

- Kerstin Hellmann
WWW.KEYMEDIAPHOTOGRAPHY.COM

- Ronan Courell
RONANVCOURELL@UTVINTERNET.COM

- Joanne Maloney
WWW.QUOTEDMOMENTS.COM

- Noel Browne
WWW.NOELBROWNEPHOTOGRAPHER.COM

- Ben Wrafter
WRAFTER@IOL.IE

Photo Contributors

– Mary Corcoran
MARYPCORCORAN@YAHOO.CO.UK

– Brian Dwyer
WWW.IMAGESBYBRIAN.NET

– Kerstin Hellmann
WWW.KEYMEDIAPHOTOGRAPHY.COM

– Kerstin Hellmann
WWW.KEYMEDIAPHOTOGRAPHY.COM

– Adele O'Byrne
ADELEOBYRNE@YAHOO.COM

– Brian Dwyer
WWW.IMAGESBYBRIAN.NET

– Derville Conroy
DERVILLE.CONROY@GMAIL.COM

– Brian Dwyer
WWW.IMAGESBYBRIAN.NET

– Derville Conroy
DERVILLE.CONROY@GMAIL.COM

– Warren Dowling
THEDOWLINGFAMILY@GMAIL.COM

– Pamela Derrig
PALLIE1@O2.IE

– Noel Browne
WWW.NOELBROWNEPHOTOGRAPHER.COM

– Dickon Whitehead
WWW.DICKONWHITEHEAD.COM

– Aafke Bakker
WWW.AMOSTLIKEABLEPLACE.WORDPRESS.COM

– Sarah Keane
KEANESARAH@MSN.COM

– Adele O'Byrne
ADELEOBYRNE@YAHOO.COM

– Karin Pritzel
WWW.PRITZELPHOTOGRAPHY.COM

– Dickon Whitehead
WWW.DICKONWHITEHEAD.COM

– Noel Browne
WWW.NOELBROWNEPHOTOGRAPHER.COM

– John Moylette
JMOYLETTE@EIRCOM.NET

– Noel Browne
WWW.NOELBROWNEPHOTOGRAPHER.COM

– Matt Loughrey
WWW.CROAGHPATRICK365.COM

Photo Contributors

– Liam Brogan
LIAM_BROGAN@HOTMAIL.COM

– Jay Meenan
WWW.REDISTUDIOS.IE

– Noel Browne
WWW.NOELBROWNEPHOTOGRAPHER.COM

– Brian Dwyer
WWW.IMAGESBYBRIAN.NET

– John Mee
WWW.JOHNMEEPHOTOGRAPHY.COM

– Kerstin Hellmann
WWW.KEYMEDIAPHOTOGRAPHY.COM

– Derville Conroy
DERVILLE.CONROY@GMAIL.COM

– Lorraine McEniry
LANIEMC@HOTMAIL.COM

– Kerstin Hellmann
WWW.KEYMEDIAPHOTOGRAPHY.COM

– Matt Loughrey
WWW.CROAGHPATRICK365.COM

– Brian Dwyer
WWW.IMAGESBYBRIAN.NET

– Brian Dwyer
WWW.IMAGESBYBRIAN.NET

– Matt Loughrey
WWW.CROAGHPATRICK365.COM

– Matt Loughrey
WWW.CROAGHPATRICK365.COM

– Jim Stapleton
WWW.FLICKR.COM/PHOTOS/JIMSTAPLETON

– Pat Maloney
PAT_MALONEY@EIRCOM.NET

– Angela McGowan
ANGELA_MCGOWAN@YAHOO.COM

– John Roche
OB1SCOBY@GMAIL.COM

– Sarah Keane
KEANESARAH@MSN.COM

– Walter Browne
WALTBROWNE@HOTMAIL.COM

– Aafke Bakker
WWW.AMOSTLIKEABLEPLACE.WORDPRESS.COM

– Val Robus
HTTP://MAGNUMLADY.COM

Photo Contributors

– Kerstin Hellmann
WWW.KEYMEDIAPHOTOGRAPHY.COM

– Matt Loughrey
WWW.CROAGHPATRICK365.COM

– Richie Hunt
BIG.POPPA.FLUFF@GMAIL.COM

– Matt Loughrey
WWW.CROAGHPATRICK365.COM

Poetry Contributors

– Peter Costello
WWW.REASONS4RHYMES.COM

– Antoinette Keane
ATJKEANE@EIRCOM.NET

Other Contributors

Quotations – Jarlath Cunningham
JARLATH5@GMAIL.COM

Copywriting – Aisling Kennedy
AISLING.KENNEDY@YAHOO.CO.UK

Title – Donal Jennings
DJENNINGS28@GMAIL.COM

IT Consultant – John Duffy
JOHNEDUFFY@GMAIL.COM

Acknowledgements

To my dearest Mum and my best friend Linda, who inspired this book, who shone the light, nudged me gently along and stood right beside me every step of the way to make this a reality.

To my wonderful Dad and beautiful sisters; Lorraine, Vivianne and Louise, for constantly being there for me and for their unconditional love, support and encouragement, always.

To my amazing friends and extended family who spurred me on and gave me their time, their hospitality, their feedback and most importantly their love when it really mattered.

To Kerstin at Key Media Design for her outstanding work, her dedication to this project and her incredible patience.

To my colleagues and more importantly my friends at KPS Colour Print for their support, professionalism, attention to detail and their team-work.

Finally I could not have completed this book without the passion of the contributors that is evident in their work, I am eternally grateful to you all.

Joanne